# PRE-WORK FOR FREED-UP FROM DEBT

**IMPORTANT**
Please read and complete the following pre-work before the first session.

# Pre-Work

## How Did You Get Here?

No matter how much debt you have, the good news is it's possible to get out from under it, and not only that — it's possible to stay out of debt forever. The step-by-step plan you're about to learn will teach you how.

It may take some time, and it will take some changes in behavior and in attitudes and beliefs. All too often, those who quickly get out of debt eventually get right back in. That's because while their financial picture improved initially, they only addressed the outward symptoms of their financial issues without tracing those symptoms back to their root causes, which often include ways of thinking about money.

This pre-work will help you identify the true causes of your debt — including behaviors and attitudes.

# What Circumstances Led to Your Debt?

Consider the circumstances below and check each one that contributed to your debt. Chances are good there was more than just one factor, so check off as many as apply.

- ❏ Unemployment
- ❏ Uninsured medical expenses
- ❏ Divorce
- ❏ Small business failure
- ❏ Couldn't find another way to pay for school
- ❏ Large unexpected expenses (home/car repairs, etc.)
- ❏ Living beyond my means
- ❏ No emergency fund
- ❏ Not using a plan (budget) to guide my spending
- ❏ Other: _____

Did you include "Living beyond my means," "No emergency fund," or "Not using a plan (budget) to guide my spending"? If so, that's not surprising. In many cases, those factors contribute to people's debt. Acknowledging them is a very positive step toward getting out of debt in a way that will give you the best chance of staying out of debt. By doing so you are taking responsibility for your debt.

You may have been through some very difficult circumstances, such as divorce or the loss of your job. But owning your role in your current situation is a very honest, healthy, and helpful step toward developing lasting solutions.

Now consider what attitudinal factors may have played a role in your financial problems.

## What Beliefs Led to Your Debt?

Look at the statements below, and check each one that applies to your situation.

- ❏ Everyone has credit card debt; it's normal, unavoidable.
  *See Proverbs 22:7, 1 Corinthians 7:23*
- ❏ Buying things makes me feel good about myself. My credit cards enable me to pick myself up when I'm not feeling so great.
  *See Luke 12:15, 1 Samuel 16:7*
- ❏ Using my credit cards gives me a sense of freedom, independence, control, or power.
  *See Matthew 6:25-34, 2 Corinthians 12:7-10, Philippians 4:19*

One of the best ways to root out a false belief is to meditate on the truth. Below each statement, there are Bible verses for that purpose.

Are there any other ways of thinking that contributed to your debt? Once you become aware of any beliefs that played a role in your debt, ask whether each one is true, productive, or God glorifying. Chances are good they are not.

*"Do not conform to the pattern of this world, but be transformed by the renewing of your mind."*
Romans 12:2

These steps — taking responsibility for your debts and identifying any attitudes or beliefs that contributed to your debts — are essential in solving your financial problems for good.

## What You'll Need

Please bring to the workshop the details of your debts, such as your most recent credit card statements and paperwork showing the terms (balance, interest rate, monthly payment) of student loans, vehicle loans, or any other debts.

Remember, no matter how much debt you have, it's possible to get out of debt and stay out of debt forever. Be encouraged by this promise from God's Word: "I can do everything through him who gives me strength" (Philippians 4:13, NIV).

# Freed-Up FROM DEBT

How to Get Out and Stay Out

# Freed-Up FROM DEBT

How to Get Out and Stay Out

PARTICIPANT'S WORKBOOK

## MATT BELL

NAVPRESS

*Freed-Up from Debt Participant's Workbook*
Copyright © 2009 by Willow Creek Association

Requests for information should be addressed to:
Willow Creek Association
67 E. Algonquin Road
South Barrington, IL 60010

ISBN: 0744198577

All Scripture quotations, unless otherwise indicated, are taken from the HOLY BIBLE, TODAY'S NEW INTERNATIONAL VERSION®. TNIV®. Copyright© 2001, 2005 by International Bible Society. Used by permission of Zondervan. All rights reserved.

Scripture quotations marked (NIV) are taken from the HOLY BIBLE, NEW INTERNATIONAL VERSION®. NIV®. Copyright © 1973, 1978, 1984 by International Bible Society. Used by permission of Zondervan. All rights reserved.

Scripture quotations marked (NLT) are taken from the Holy Bible, New Living Translation, copyright 1996, 2004. Used by permission of Tyndale House Publishers, Inc., Wheaton, Illinois 60189. All rights reserved.

All rights reserved. No part of this publication may be reproduced, stored in a retrieval system, or transmitted in any form or by any means – electronic, mechanical, photocopy, recording, or any other – except for brief quotations in printed reviews, without the prior permission of the publisher.

Cover and interior design by Daab Creative

Printed in the United States of America

09 10 11 12 13 14 15 • 10 9 8 7 6 5 4 3 2 1

# Contents

Foreword .................................. 12

Acknowledgements .................... 13

Session 1 .................................. 14

Session 2 .................................. 27

Appendix .................................. 43

**FACILITATOR'S NOTE:** This course can be used by individuals, in a small group or presented as a workshop. In the latter two cases it is helpful to have a Facilitator. A free Facilitator's Guide can be found at www.goodsenseministry.com. Go to the RESOURCES link and download the *Freed-Up from Debt Facilitator's Guide*.

# Foreword

Debt is so common in our culture that it feels normal, unavoidable. It has become an accepted way of life to carry a balance on credit cards, finance vehicles, and stretch as far as possible when buying a home. But following this well-traveled path comes with a cost that goes far beyond all of the interest payments. It can take a toll on our relationships, health, and even our faith. I know. I once had $20,000 of credit card debt and a car payment.

By participating in this workshop, you've chosen a different path. By deciding to do something about your debts you've chosen to dial down the financial stress in your life. You've chosen financial freedom over financial bondage. And you've chosen to put yourself in a better position to hear and respond to God's call on your life.

Follow the steps outlined in this resource and you will get out of debt. It probably won't happen overnight, but it will happen. And I believe God will honor your commitment, providing you with the encouragement you need to succeed.

May God guide you and bless you on your journey out of debt.

Matt Bell

# Acknowledgements

The ideas in this resource came about through personal experience, research, and the invaluable input from numerous dedicated stewardship leaders from around the country. My thanks to Brad Brestel, David Briggs, Chris DeGraff, Skip and Catherine Galanes, Jim Grubb, Leo Sabo, and Dick Towner. This team of reviewers made many helpful suggestions for improvement, caught several errors, and otherwise helped craft this into a far better resource than it would have been otherwise.

Thanks as well to the talented team of producers, editors, and video production team members involved in this project, including: Stephanie Oakley, Bob Gustafson, Erica Dekker, Sarah Trommer, Lucas Mroz, Dave Olson, Chris Scherf, Peter Kosmal, and Tim Giardino.

# SESSION 1

# Matt's Story

## Activity

*Take a few moments and reflect on the following questions. If you want, write down your answers in the space provided.*

1. Why do you want to be out of debt?

2. What could you accomplish if you were free of debt?

3. What goals or dreams has God placed on your heart that if you were out of debt, you'd have a much better chance of accomplishing?

# The Word on Debt

## Biblical Principle #1

**The Bible does not say that going into debt is a sin, but it cautions that debt can enslave us.**

*"The borrower is servant to the lender."*
PROVERBS 22:7 (NIV)

*"Money is a terrible master, but an excellent servant."*
— CIRCUS FOUNDER P.T. BARNUM

- Money can be an excellent servant when we get the power of compound interest working for us.

- Compound interest is the process in which invested money earns interest, and then that interest earns more interest, and so on.

- When compound interest works against you (debt), it's a disaster.

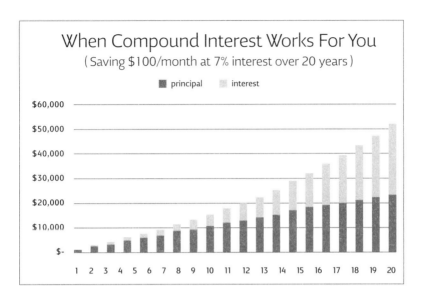

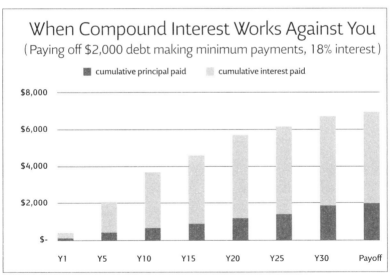

SESSION ONE

# Biblical Principle #2

## We need to repay our debts.

- Psalm 37:21 says that people who borrow and do not repay are "wicked."

- There are some situations where bankruptcy may be the only viable alternative, but we are to do all that we can to repay our debts.

*See page 45 in the appendix for more information on bankruptcy.*

# Biblical Principle #3

## We are not to presume upon the future.

*"Now listen, you who say, 'Today or tomorrow we will go to this or that city, spend a year there, carry on business and make money.' Why, you do not even know what will happen tomorrow. What is your life? You are a mist that appears for a little while and then vanishes. Instead, you ought to say, 'If it is the Lord's will, we will live and do this or that.'"*
JAMES 4:13-15

- If you use a credit card, you need to have the full amount of the purchase that day so you can pay in full when the bill comes.

- If you take out a mortgage to buy a house, the payments have to be truly affordable.

# Biblical Principle #4

**Borrowing money can interfere with the relationship God intended to have with us.**

- God knows our needs and promises to provide for us — all He asks is that we make Him our highest priority (Matthew 6).

- A credit card gives us the godlike ability to buy anything we want, any time we want.

- God may plan to give you the very thing you're tempted to buy on credit if you'll simply wait.

- If you're going to use credit, especially to make a major purchase, pray over the decision and take your time.

## Activity

*How has your debt impacted your relationship with God? Take a few minutes and write some thoughts.*

# The Plan

## Step 1: Go No Further into Debt

- If you're carrying a balance on a credit card, cut it up!

- Pay for purchases with cash, and if you absolutely need to use plastic, use a debit card.

- If you're making payments on a vehicle, keep that vehicle until it's paid off and until you have enough money in savings to buy your next vehicle with cash.

## *Activity*

*If you have a balance on a credit card that you don't pay in full each month, open up your wallet or purse and take it out. If you have scissors, cut it up right now, or put it in your pocket so you'll remember to do it later today.*

*See page 48 in the appendix for four guidelines for the wise use of credit cards.*

# Step 2: Find Out Where You Are Right Now

## Debt Organizer Sample: Shari

| CREDITOR | TOTAL BALANCE | INTEREST RATE (APR) | MONTHLY PAYMENT |
|---|---|---|---|
| MasterCard | $500 | 10% | $15 |
| Retail Store | $1,200 | 9% | $48 |
| Visa | $1,800 | 18% | $36 |
| Car Loan | $12,505 | 7% | $396 |
| **TOTALS** | $16,005 | – | $495 |

# Activity

*Use the statements and documents you gathered during your Pre-Work to enter all the details of your debts in the Debt Organizer on the following page.*

*See page 49 in the appendix for information on accelerating the payoff of a mortgage.*

## Your Debt Organizer

| CREDITOR | TOTAL BALANCE | INTEREST RATE (APR) | MONTHLY PAYMENT |
|---|---|---|---|
|  |  |  |  |
|  |  |  |  |
|  |  |  |  |
|  |  |  |  |
|  |  |  |  |
|  |  |  |  |
|  |  |  |  |
| TOTALS |  | - - - |  |

# Step 3: Request Lower Rates

- In one study, more than half of the people who called their credit card companies to request a lower interest rate were successful, and on average they lowered their rate by more than one-third.[1]

- Lower rates can have a big impact on how fast you can get out of debt.

- Assuming you've been on time with your payments, once you get a customer service representative on the phone, just say something like this:

> **PHONE SCRIPT**
> "I believe I've been a good customer, and I'd like to keep my business with you. However, I need some help on the interest rate. Is there anything you can do for me?"
> If the first person you speak with turns you down, ask to speak with a supervisor and repeat your request.
> If you have received a pre-approved offer in the mail for a card with a lower interest rate than the one you're calling about, say: "I have a pre-approval offer in front of me for a credit card with a _____ percent rate from [name of credit card company]. Can you at least match that?"

---

[1] Source: Bradley Dakake, "Deflate Your Rate: How to Lower Your Credit Card APR," Massachusetts Public Interest Research Group, http://www.masspirg.org/static/deflatereport.pdf.

- If you're successful in lowering one or more of your rates, make that change on your Debt Organizer.

*See page 50 in the appendix for how to get interest rates lowered on vehicle and education loans.*

## Activity

*Take a few minutes now and review your Debt Organizer on page 24. Look at your list of creditors and the interest rates they're charging. Star or circle at least one that you will commit to calling to request a lower rate.*

# SESSION 2

# The Plan, continued

## Step 4: Fix and Roll Your Payments

### Fix

- Your minimum payment is based on a percentage of your balance, so if your balance declines a little each month, your minimum due will decline as well.

- Paying the declining minimum due will keep you in debt for a long time.

- Instead of making the declining minimum payment each month, fix your payments on the amount that's due this month.

- You'll get out of debt a lot faster without spending any more on debt payments than you are right now.

### Roll

- Once one debt is paid in full, take the full amount you were paying on that bill and roll it into the debt that currently has the lowest balance.

## Step 5: Accelerate Your Payments

- If you can find some extra money — an "accelerator" — to apply to your debts, you'll get out of debt even faster.

- The debt with the lowest balance should get the accelerator.

- When the first debt is paid off, the accelerator should be applied to the debt with the next lowest balance.

- Adding $50 a month to your debt payments only takes finding less than $1.70 per day.

*Activity*

*Earlier you filled in your Debt Organizer (page 24). Now use that information to fill in the Debt Elimination Plan on page 30.*

*Begin by listing your debts again, this time in order from lowest to highest balance. Then add an accelerator amount to the debt with the lowest balance. You may have no idea how much extra money — $25 or $50 or $100 — you could come up with. For now, just set a goal in faith.*

## Your Debt Elimination Plan

| CREDITOR | TOTAL BALANCE | INTEREST RATE (APR) | MONTHLY PAYMENT (FIXED) |
|---|---|---|---|
|  |  |  |  |
|  |  |  |  |
|  |  |  |  |
|  |  |  |  |
|  |  |  |  |
| TOTALS |  | --- |  |

## Three Ways to Find an Accelerator

*"Do not withhold good from those to whom it is due,*
   *when it is in your power to act.*
 *Do not say to your neighbor,*
   *'Come back tomorrow and I'll give it to you' —*
   *when you already have it with you."*
PROVERBS 3:27-28

- Sell stuff.

   » Look through your attic, basement, garage, and closets for items you haven't used in the last six to 12 months.

   » Hold a garage sale or sell your stuff online.

   » Use the money you make to pay down debt.

- Spend smarter.

  » You need a Cash Flow Plan (budget) and a way to track your expenses so you know where your money is going.

  » A budget is the single most powerful practical tool anyone can use to manage money more effectively.

  *See page 51 in the appendix for more on setting up and using a Cash Flow Plan.*

  » Housing

  *See page 53 in the appendix for how to calculate the percentage of your monthly gross income that you spend on housing.*

  - Spend no more than 25 percent of your monthly gross income on housing.

    - If you own, that includes mortgage, taxes, and insurance.

    - If you rent, that includes rent and renter's insurance.

- If you spend more than 25 percent:

    - If you're a renter, consider taking in a roommate.

    - If you own, consider selling your house and moving to a more affordable house.

» Transportation

  - Consider going from a two-car household to one-car household.

  - Consider if you could get by without a car for a season, commuting with a friend to work or taking public transportation.

  - Find out the cost savings of raising the deductible on your vehicle insurance, but don't do this unless you have an emergency fund in place.

» Food

- Shop with a list.

- Find out which stores have the best prices on items you buy regularly.

- Use coupons.

   *See page 54 in the appendix for coupon tips and a Web site that helps you use coupons more effectively.*

» Consider going on a spending fast by not spending money on certain categories for a period of time.

- You might decide not to buy clothes or spend money on entertainment for six months, or you might decide to buy only essential groceries.

- Find someone who's willing to go on the spending fast with you.

- Increase your income.

  » Take on a part-time job for a few evenings a week or on weekends.

  *See page 55 in the appendix for information on a free online calculator that allows you to try various accelerator amounts to see how quickly you could get out of debt.*

## Emergency Fund

- If you don't have an emergency fund, fix your monthly payments on today's minimum required payments, and then use the accelerator to save enough to cover one month of living expenses.

- After you get out of debt, build that emergency fund up to at least six months' worth of living expenses.

  *See page 57 in the appendix for help in calculating one month's worth of living expenses.*

## Activity

*Think about the three ways to find an accelerator.*
*Which could you implement?*

- ❏ *Sell some possessions.*
- ❏ *Spend more effectively.*
- ❏ *Increase income.*

*Get specific. What could you sell? In which categories could you spend more effectively? How much time could you devote to a part-time job, and where could you apply?*

*Now refer back to the accelerator you added to your Debt Elimination Plan. With these ideas in mind, could you increase that amount? If so, write in the new amount on your Debt Elimination Plan (p. 30).*

## Step 6: Make a Commitment

- Research has shown that the simple act of signing your name to a commitment greatly improves your chances of following through on that commitment.

- Don't sign the form out of a sense of pressure — do it because it is your heartfelt desire and commitment to get and stay out of debt.

## *Activity*

*Fill out the commitment form below:*

*Commitment Form*

*On this _____ day of _____ (month), _____ (year), I/we commit to going no further into debt, to doing everything possible to get out and stay out of consumer debt, and to praying regularly for God's guidance and encouragement.*

*Signed* _____

_____

# Step 7: Go Public with Your Commitment

*"Two are better than one,
because they have a good return for their labor:
If they fall down,
they can help each other up.
But pity those who fall
and have no one to help them up!"*
Ecclesiastes 4:9-10

- Think of two trusted friends or relatives to go public with about your commitment to get out of debt.

- If you're married, count your spouse as one person you've gone public with, but each of you should choose one additional person.

- Your role is to tell your accountability partners the details of your debts and your commitment to getting and staying out of debt.

- Their role is to know and ask about your situation and to encourage and pray for you.

- This may be uncomfortable, but it is one of the most important factors in your success.

# Activity

*Write down the names of two potential accountability partners. If you have their number with you, take time right now to contact them.*

Names:

# Staying Out of Debt Forever

- Use a Cash Flow Plan.

- Maintain a reserve (emergency fund).

- Never forget who you are.

    » Our culture calls us consumers, but to consume literally means to use up, spend wastefully, and squander.

    » God didn't create us to be consumers — He made man and woman in His image.

    » There is no such thing as a Christian consumer.

    » Financially, the Bible describes us as stewards.

    - Our responsibility is to manage well what God has entrusted to our care.

    - When we understand our purpose and who God made us to be, debt simply makes no sense.

# Activity

*You've heard some steps you can implement even now to make sure that once you've gotten out of debt, you stay out. Now, write down at least one action step you will take.*

# The Larger Purpose for Your Debt

- When you feel discouraged about your debts, look for the largest purpose for your situation.

*"… in order to keep me from becoming conceited, I was given a thorn in my flesh, a messenger of Satan, to torment me. Three times I pleaded with the Lord to take it away from me. But he said to me, 'My grace is sufficient for you, for my power is made perfect in weakness.'"*
2 Corinthians 12:7-9

- Look to see how God is using your debt to further build your character, strengthen your faith, and be an encouragement and help to others.

- It's likely that your situation is really about more than money.

# APPENDIX

# Contents

Bankruptcy: An Option of Last Resort ................. 45

How to Use Credit Cards Wisely .......................... 48

Accelerating Mortgage Payoff .............................. 49

Getting Interest Rates Lowered
on Vehicle and Education Loans .......................... 50

Using a Cash Flow Plan ........................................ 51

Managing Housing Costs ..................................... 53

Money-Saving Web Sites ...................................... 54

Debt Calculator .................................................... 55

Calculating Living Expenses
for an Emergency Fund ....................................... 57

What About Giving? ............................................ 58

Buying Vehicles .................................................... 59

More Debt Solutions ............................................ 60

Debt Solution Watch-Outs .................................. 61

# Bankruptcy: An Option of Last Resort

If you're thinking about filing for bankruptcy, here are three questions that will help you determine whether it's the right step for you. Before filing for bankruptcy, you should be able to say yes to all three questions.

## 1) Is there no other choice?

Have you truly done all that you can to free up money to pay your debts? Have you considered even the "crazy" ideas like selling your house or going from a two-car family to a one-car family? Have you negotiated with your creditors in good faith only to have them play hardball by garnishing your wages? Have you sought the assistance of a budget counselor through your church's financial ministry, such as Good $ense (www.goodsenseministry.com), or Crown Financial Ministries (www.crown.org)? Have you talked about your situation with a credit counselor affiliated with the National Foundation for Credit Counseling (www.debtadvice.org)?

If you have done everything that is "in your power to act" (see Proverbs 3:27-28) and still find it impossible to pay your debts, bankruptcy may be your only alternative.

## 2) Have you taken responsibility for your debts?

You may have gone through some difficult circumstances that contributed to your debts — the death of a spouse, a divorce, or an extended time of unemployment. Still, chances are you can identify something you could have done to avoid the financial problems you now face, or at least to make them less severe. Owning up to your part in the situation is essential if you are to truly solve your financial problems. What could you have done differently?

## 3) Have you taken steps to avoid future debt problems?

If you weren't using a cash flow plan prior to getting into debt, are you now using one? If any of your debts are credit card debts, have you stopped using your credit cards? Do you have an accountability partner you are meeting with on a regular basis to review your finances?

## What Bankruptcy Can and Cannot Do

There are certain debts and ongoing obligations that cannot be wiped out through bankruptcy. If you're making child-support or alimony payments, you'll need to keep making those payments. If you are behind on such support, you'll need to catch up; such debts are never dischargeable. Student loans are rarely forgiven. Many tax debts are not dischargeable. If you have a home or vehicle you'd like to keep, in many cases you will need to continue making your payments.

Filing for bankruptcy stops most debt collectors from contacting you. It also means that your creditors may not sue you or proceed with a pending lawsuit, put liens on your property, seize your property, or garnish your wages to pay your debts. Whether foreclosure proceedings will continue depends on what type of bankruptcy you file. Under Chapter 7, such proceedings are stopped initially; however, in many cases they eventually will be allowed to continue. Under Chapter 13, foreclosure proceedings will be stopped; however, you will need to make up missed payments as part of a repayment plan.

Within the six-month period prior to filing for bankruptcy, you will need to complete credit counseling in order to determine whether you really need to go through bankruptcy. If you end up filing, you will also have to take part in a personal money-management course.

## Types of Bankruptcy

The most common types of bankruptcy for individuals are Chapter 7 and Chapter 13, named for sections of the bankruptcy code.

Chapter 7 is known as liquidation bankruptcy. You give up certain nonexempt assets, which are sold in order to pay as much of your unsecured debt (credit card debt, medical debt, etc.) as possible. Many exemptions vary by state, but retirement accounts, Social Security, unemployment, and disability income are federally exempt. Whatever unsecured debts remain are then forgiven, except for the debts mentioned earlier, such as student loan debt and many tax debts.

You will be eligible for Chapter 7 if your average monthly income from the last six months is below the median for your household size in your state (go to www.usdoj.gov/ust and click on "Means Testing Information"). If it is not below the median, you'll have to take a "means test." There's a free means test calculator at www.legalconsumer.com.

With a Chapter 13 bankruptcy, a court-approved plan will dictate the repayment of some or all of your debts over three to five years. You must devote all of your disposable income (defined as your average monthly income from the past six months, minus monthly expense amounts as allowed by the Bankruptcy Code) to the plan.

# Next Steps

While some people opt for a do-it-yourself bankruptcy, you will probably be better off working with an attorney who specializes in bankruptcy law. Ask for a referral from an attorney you know or check with the American Board of Certification (www.abcworld.org) or the National Association of Consumer Bankruptcy Attorneys (www.nacba.org).

# How to Use Credit Cards Wisely

If you currently are not paying off your balance every month on a credit card, you should absolutely stop using credit cards. When deciding whether or not to use credit cards again after you are out of debt, the key is to know yourself and see if you can adhere to the following guidelines.

### 1) Only use a credit card to spend planned amounts.

If your Cash Flow Plan allows you to spend $100 on clothing each month, you can use a credit card to charge $100 worth of clothing.

### 2) Record your credit card spending as you use your card.

If you're tracking spending with a paper-and-pencil system, whenever you charge a purchase, write it down on the day you make that purchase. Electronic budget tools make this fairly easy.

### 3) Pay your balance in full each month.

### 4) If you can't adhere to these rules, don't use credit cards.

# Accelerating Mortgage Payoff

If you'd like to accelerate the payoff of your mortgage, use the Accelerated Debt Payoff Calculator found on www.moneypurposejoy.com (click on "Resources," then "Calculators," then "Accelerated Debt Payoff Calculator.") to see how much more quickly your mortgage will be retired using various added payment amounts.

First, contact your mortgage lender to find out the current balance on your loan and enter that amount along with the interest rate and monthly payment (principal and interest only — don't include your taxes or insurance).

Next, add various amounts you could add to your monthly payment to see how much more quickly you'll be out of debt and how much less you'll pay in interest.

It's best to write a separate check for the added amount you are paying on your mortgage and include a note to your lender indicating that it is to be applied to the principal on the loan. Also check to be sure your contract does not contain a penalty for the early payoff of your mortgage.

# Getting Interest Rates Lowered on Vehicle and Education Loans

## Vehicle Loans

If interest rates on vehicle loans have dropped (check www.bankrate.com), look into refinancing. To qualify, your car may need to be less than five years old, and your car will need to be worth more than what you owe. When looking for a loan, check with your current financing company, but then shop around. Credit unions often offer the best rates.

## Education Loans

If you have one or more student loans guaranteed by the federal government, you may qualify to "consolidate" even one loan at a lower interest rate. For more information about loan consolidation, go to www.loanconsolidation.ed.gov.

# Using a Cash Flow Plan

A Cash Flow Plan is one of the most powerful, practical tools for managing money well, and it is an essential tool for getting and staying out of debt. You can download a blank plan from www.moneypurposejoy.com by clicking on "Resources" and then "Downloads." Here's how to set up and use a Cash Flow Plan.

## 1) Estimate current income and expenses.

Fill out the "Now" columns of the Monthly Cash Flow Plan, starting with your household's monthly gross income — the amount before deductions. Next, enter your current monthly giving, saving, and debt payments. Then fill in the rest of the "Now" figures as well as you can. You may have no idea how much you're spending in a certain category. That's OK. For now, just make an educated guess.

Note that the first line in each section is for the total of the section. Be sure to fill in the last three lines: your total monthly income, total monthly expenses, and the difference between the two.

## 2) Plan future income and expenses.

Once you're done with the "Now" columns, fill in the "Goal" columns. In most cases, your income goal will be the same as your current income — that is, unless you plan to try to increase your income. If you feel led to make any changes in how much you give each month, enter the new amount. If you have no emergency fund savings, before accelerating debt payments, set a goal to save something each month until you have one month's worth of living expenses set aside. After that, set an "accelerator" goal — an amount to add to your minimum monthly debt payments to speed up the process of becoming debt-free. Add that figure to the monthly amount you're now paying on the lowest balance debt and put the new amount in the "Goal" column. Then transfer the "Now" numbers from your other debts into the "Goal" column. Set goals in the rest of the spending categories in a way that leaves you with a balanced plan. "Income minus Expenses" should equal zero.

Now transfer your income and spending goals from the Monthly Cash Flow Plan to the "Goals" row at the top of the Monthly Cash Flow Tracker (download at www.moneypurposejoy.com).

## 3) Track actual income and expenses.

As you spend money, keep your receipts or jot down how much you spend on a notepad. At the end of each day, enter your expenditures in the Monthly Cash Flow Tracker. At the bottom of the form are the numbers 1 through 31, representing the days of the month. After entering your income and expenses for the day, put a line through the date. That'll be an indicator that you recorded the day's activity.

## 4) Review results versus plan.

At the end of each month, total your income and your expenditures for each spending category and compare the results with your goals. Identify areas to improve.

Remember, a Cash Flow Plan is not about less. It's about more — having more knowledge of where your money is going, so you can spend more effectively, so that you have more for what really matters — like getting out of debt as soon as possible!

# Managing Housing Costs

If you're having a tough time making your mortgage payments, the first step is to assess whether you could afford your home under somewhat better terms, such as a lower interest rate.

A good guideline is to devote no more than 25 percent of your monthly gross income to the combination of your mortgage principal and interest, property taxes, and insurance. What percentage of your gross monthly income are you paying for housing?

($ _____ ) + ($ _____ ) + ($ _____ ) = ($ _____ ) / ($ _____ ) = _____ %
MONTHLY MORTGAGE PAYMENT — MONTHLY PROPERTY TAXES — MONTHLY INSURANCE PREMIUM — MONTHLY TOTAL — MONTHLY GROSS INCOME

If you're spending much more than 25 percent of your monthly gross income on housing, compare your interest rate with current rates (check www.bankrate.com). If today's rates are better than what you're paying and you have equity in your home, contact a mortgage broker to see about refinancing.

If you're in a hardship situation (e.g. you owe more on your house than it's worth and are struggling under the weight of other debts), go to www.makinghomeaffordable.gov to see if you may qualify for government subsidized loan modification. Another good next step is to get in touch with a trained housing counselor certified by the U.S. Department of Housing and Urban Development (HUD) either at www.hud.gov/foreclosure or www.HousingHelpNow.org.

# Money-Saving Web Sites

**TIPS FOR USING GROCERY COUPONS MORE EFFECTIVELY**

www.couponmom.com

**COMPARE PRICES**

www.shopzilla.com
www.shopping.com

**FIND COUPON CODES**

www.couponcabin.com
www.retailmenot.com

**SAVE ON ENTERTAINMENT**

www.restaurant.com

**EARN REBATES**

www.ebates.com

**CREATE A GIFT-GIVING BUDGET**

www.moneypurposejoy.com
(Click on "Resources," then "Downloads.")

**SEE IF YOU'RE HAVING TOO MUCH TAX WITHHELD FROM YOUR PAYCHECK**

www.irs.gov
(Search for "Withholding Calculator.")

**FIND A "SWAP" WHERE YOU CAN TRADE CLOTHING, KIDS' ITEMS, ETC.**

www.meetup.com

**ONGOING IDEAS**

www.moneypurposejoy.com

# Debt Calculator

To see how much more quickly you'll be out of debt under various debt repayment scenarios, go to www.moneypurposejoy.com, click on "Resources," "Calculators," and then "Accelerated Debt Payoff Calculator."

1) Starting with your smallest balance debt, enter the information for all of your debts.

You do not need to include your mortgage, but if you do want to accelerate pay-off of your mortgage, do include your mortgage and see the tips on page 49.

2) Enter 0 for the amount you could add to your debt payoff plan and then hit "Calculate Results."

3) Take the information from the "Current Totals" line and enter it on the "Fixed Payments" line on the next page.

This is how long it will take you to pay off your debts and how much interest you will pay if you "fix" your payments on today's minimum required payments. In other words, if your required payment on a debt this month is $45, the assumption is that you will continue paying $45 each month.

4) Take the numbers from the "ADP Totals" line and write them on the "Fix & Roll" line below.

Under this scenario, the assumption is that once one debt is paid off you will take the full amount you were paying on that debt and roll it over to the next lowest balance debt.

5) Calculate the results when adding different monthly amounts to your debt payoff plan.

| PAYOFF METHOD | COUNTDOWN TO FREEDOM | INTEREST |
|---|---|---|
| Fixed Payments | _____ Months | $ _____ |
| Fix & Roll | _____ Months | $ _____ |
| $25 Accelerator | _____ Months | $ _____ |
| $50 Accelerator | _____ Months | $ _____ |
| $ _____ Accelerator | _____ Months | $ _____ |

# Calculating Living Expenses for an Emergency Fund

While there are very few certainties in life, one of them is that we can expect unexpected expenses. That's why it's important to maintain an emergency fund.

Before accelerating your debt payments, build an emergency fund totaling one month's worth of living expenses. To figure out how much that is, go through your Cash Flow Plan and add up all of the monthly expenses that would remain if you were to lose your job today. Some expenses might go away or at least decrease. You won't absolutely need to spend money on entertainment, for example. But you will need to keep making the payments for your mortgage, utilities, insurance, etc.

Once you know how much you would need to live on for a month, that's your emergency fund savings goal. Use whatever accelerator money you're able to free up through more effective spending, selling unused possessions, or taking on a temporary part-time job to build this base of savings. Good places to keep this money include a bank (traditional or online) or credit union savings or money market account.

After you're out of debt, build this emergency fund up to six months' worth of living expenses.

# What About Giving?

As followers of Christ, the Bible teaches us to make generosity our highest financial priority (Proverbs 3:9).

It isn't that God needs our money (Psalm 50:12); it's that He wants our hearts. When we give to Christ-centered causes we express very tangibly that our relationship with Christ is our highest priority (Matthew 6:19-24). Giving to support God's work in the world keeps our hearts focused on God.

The Bible also teaches very consistently that there are blessings that flow from generosity. Proverbs 11:24 states, "One person gives freely, yet gains even more; another withholds unduly, but comes to poverty." And 2 Corinthians 9:6 says, "Whoever sows sparingly will also reap sparingly, and whoever sows generously will also reap generously." We are not to give motivated by a desire for gain; however, it's a foundational spiritual principle that there are blessings that flow from generosity. Sometimes there are material blessings, sometimes other types of blessings.

For these reasons, explore other ways to free up money for debt repayment before considering any changes in how much you give. Could you go from a two-car household to a one-car household, sell unused possessions, take in a roommate, or temporarily take on a part-time job?

Ultimately, your decision about how much to give is between you and God. But always give something, and give at a level that for you represents what the Bible calls a "first fruits" gift — that's a first-priority gift, a choice gift.

# Buying Vehicles

The average new car is reliable for 12 years or 130,000 miles.[2] If you keep up with the basic maintenance, like regular oil changes, most cars will be reliable for longer than that. Commit today to keeping your vehicles longer — at least 10 years, preferably longer — and you'll be able to break the cycle of financing vehicles forever.

If you currently have a vehicle payment, once the vehicle is paid off, keep making those payments. Just send them to a savings account.

When you're ready to purchase your next vehicle, here are two Web sites that will help:

### CONSUMERREPORTS.ORG

While there is some advice you can get for free on the site, paying for one month's worth of full access will enable you to read vehicle reviews, get the magazine's unbiased opinions as to which cars are the best values within various price ranges, and see which ones are most likely to last 200,000 miles.

### EDMUNDS.COM

Search for the "True Cost to Own" tool, which enables you to review various vehicles' estimated annual costs for maintenance, repairs, fuel, insurance, and more.

---

[2]  Source: U.S. Department of Transportation

# More Debt Solutions

If you've tried all of the steps outlined in this workshop and are still struggling to pay your bills, here are some additional options.

## Credit Card Debt

Find a nearby credit-counseling agency via www.DebtAdvice.org and ask about a debt-management plan.

## Medical Debt

Call your medical provider's financial aid office and ask about a no-interest payment plan.

## Student Loan Debt

Learn about income-based repayment plans, deferment, forbearance, and forgiveness at www.finaid.org and also www.studentaid.ed.gov.

## Tax Debt

File your return and pay as much as you can. Then look into an installment plan at www.irs.gov (click on "I need to…" and then choose "Set Up a Payment Plan").

## Vehicle Debt

Ask your lender about a loan modification or extension (skipping a payment that is then added to the end of your loan). If you are leasing, look into a lease assumption at www.leasetrader.com or www.swapalease.com.

# Debt Solution Watch-Outs

## Debt Settlement Companies

Such companies purport to lower your balances. They often advise people to stop making payments to their creditors and to send them the money instead. They say they will save the money until they have enough to make a settlement offer. But there's no guarantee that a creditor will accept the offer. Plus, not paying your debts will make your balances grow, your credit score drop, and put you at risk of being sued. The best advice is to steer clear of debt settlement companies.

## Zero Percent Balance Transfers

Watch out for balance transfer fees, short introductory periods after which the rate increases, stiff penalties for late payments, and other restrictive rules and regulations buried in the fine print.

## Borrowing Against Your Home Equity

Trading high-interest credit card debt for a lower-cost home equity loan, with potentially tax deductible interest, may sound tempting. But you would be trading unsecured debt for secured debt. If you had to take the extreme step of filing for bankruptcy, your unsecured debt may be dismissed; however, a home equity loan is secured by your house. If you can't make the payments, you could lose your house.

# Borrowing Against a Retirement Plan

**EMPLOYER-SPONSORED PLAN**

One issue in borrowing against an employer-sponsored plan such as a 401(k) or 403(b) is that if you leave your job for any reason, the loan will become due, often within 30 to 90 days. If you don't repay the money, the balance is taxed and penalized as an early distribution.

Hardship withdrawals may be available if there is an "immediate and heavy financial need." However, in most cases you will need to pay taxes on the money, and if you are under 59 ½, a 10 percent penalty. You can make a penalty-free withdrawal if:

- You become totally disabled.

- You are in debt for medical expenses that exceed 7.5 percent of your adjusted gross income.

- You are required by court order to give the money to your divorced spouse, a child, or a dependent.

- You leave your employer at age 55 or later due to permanent layoff, termination, quitting, or taking early retirement.

**TRADITIONAL INDIVIDUAL RETIREMENT ACCOUNT (IRA)**

If you take money out of a traditional IRA before age 59 ½, you will typically owe taxes and a 10 percent penalty because it will be considered a premature distribution. The following hardships qualify for penalty-free (but not tax-free) early distributions:

- Total and permanent disability

- Excessive unreimbursed medical expenses

- Payment of medical insurance premiums while unemployed

### ROTH IRA

You may access the money you contributed to a Roth IRA (but not the earnings) for any reason without taxes or penalty at any time. While this may sound like a painless way to access money for debt repayment, doing so may hinder your ability to fund your retirement.

# Successfully navigate financial challenges and position yourself for lasting success!

Matt Bell's Money Strategies for Tough Times
Matt Bell
978-1-60006-664-1

*Matt Bell's Money Strategies for Tough Times* is specially prepared to help you handle (and prevent) the tough times. Practical, proven, sound money strategies, built on the timeless foundation of God's Word, can help you take charge of your financial life.

Learn how to:

- Get out of consumer debt — for good
- Free up money through smarter spending
- Survive unemployment
- Deal with debt collectors and prevent foreclosure
- Choose the best options to pay off debts

To order copies, call NavPress at 1-800-366-7788 or log on to www.navpress.com.